AUGUST 50 COLORING PAGES
FOR ADULTS RELAXATION

SHIH CHIEN HUA

PUBLISHED BY:
SHIH CHIEN HUA
Copyright © 2018

SEABIRD SHOP >50FOR

FB FAN PAGE

Disclaimer
The information contained in this book is for general information purposes only. The information is provided by the authors and while we endeavor to keep the information up to date and correct, we make no representations or warranties of any kind, express or implied, about the completeness, accuracy, reliability, suitability or availability with respect to the book or the information, products, services, or related graphics contained in the book for any purpose. Any reliance you place on such information is therefore strictly at your own risk.

AUGUST 1ST

note:

_____

_____

_____

AUGUST 2ND

note:

_____

_____

_____

AUGUST 3RD

note:

_____

_____

_____

AUGUST 4TH

note:

_____

_____

_____

AUGUST 5TH

note:

_____

_____

_____

AUGUST 6TH

note:

_____

_____

_____

AUGUST 7TH

note:

_____

_____

_____

AUGUST 8TH

note:

_____

_____

_____

AUGUST 9TH

note:

_____

_____

_____

AUGUST 10TH

note:

_____

_____

_____

AUGUST 11TH

note:

_____

_____

_____

AUGUST 12TH

note:

_____

_____

_____

AUGUST 13TH

note:

_____

_____

_____

AUGUST 14TH

note:

_____

_____

_____

AUGUST 15TH

note:

_____

_____

_____

AUGUST 16TH

note:

_____

_____

_____

AUGUST 17TH

note:

_____

_____

_____

AUGUST 18TH

note:

_____

_____

_____

AUGUST 19TH

note:

_____

_____

_____

AUGUST 20TH

note:

_____

_____

_____

AUGUST 21TH

note:

_____

_____

_____

AUGUST 22TH

note:

_____

_____

_____

AUGUST 23TH

note:

_____

_____

_____

AUGUST 24TH

note:

_____

_____

_____

AUGUST 25TH

note:

_____

_____

_____

AUGUST 26TH

note:

_____

_____

_____

AUGUST 27TH

note:

_____

_____

_____

AUGUST 28TH

note:

_____

_____

_____

AUGUST 29TH

note:

_____

_____

_____

AUGUST 30TH

note:

_____

_____

_____

AUGUST 31TH

note:

_____

_____

_____

AUGUST 32TH

note:

_____

_____

_____

AUGUST 33TH

note:

_____

_____

_____

AUGUST 34TH

note:

_____

_____

_____

AUGUST 35TH

note:

_____

_____

_____

AUGUST 36TH

note:

_____

_____

_____

AUGUST 37TH

note:

_____

_____

_____

AUGUST 38TH

note:

_____

_____

_____

AUGUST 39TH

note:

_____

_____

_____

AUGUST 40TH

note:

_____

_____

_____

AUGUST 41TH

note:

_____

_____

_____

AUGUST 42TH

note:

_____

_____

_____

AUGUST 43TH

note:

_____

_____

_____

AUGUST 44TH

note:

_____

_____

_____

AUGUST 45TH

note:

_____

_____

_____

AUGUST 46TH

note:

_____

_____

_____

AUGUST 47TH

note:

_____

_____

_____

AUGUST 48TH

note:

_____

_____

_____

AUGUST 49TH

note:

_____

_____

_____

AUGUST 50TH

note:

_____

_____

_____

www.ingramcontent.com/pod-product-compliance
Lightning Source LLC
Chambersburg PA
CBHW081604220526
45468CB00010B/2770